REA

Beyond Self

108
KOREAN
ZEN
POEMS
by KO UN

Translated from the Korean
by Young-Moo Kim
and Brother Anthony

Parallax Press
Berkeley, California

Parallax Press
P.O. Box 7355
Berkeley, California 94707

Copyright © 1997, by Ko Un
All Rights Reserved
Printed in the United States of America

Cover and text design by Legacy Media, Inc.
Cover calligraphy by the author
Translated from the Korean by Young-Moo Kim and
Brother Anthony

Library of Congress Cataloging-in-Publication Data
    Ko, Un, 1933-
    Beyond Self : 108 Korean Zen poems / Ko Un; translat-
ed from the Korean by Young-Moo Kim and Brother
Anthony; forewords by Allen Ginsberg and Thich Nhat
Hanh; introduction by Ok-Koo Kang Grosjean; preface by
Ko Un.

    p. cm.
    ISBN 0-938077-99-6 (paperback)
    1. Zen poetry, Korean. I. Title.
PL992.42.U5B48 1997   97-523
895.7' 14—DC21   CIP

1 2 3 4 5 6 7 8 9 10 / 01 00 99 98 97

Contents

Foreword
by Allen Ginsberg

I met Ko Un in Seoul 1989 at a poetry reading. A precocious scholar, then conscripted Peoples Army worker, then alms begging monk ten years, then Buddhist Newspaper Editor-in-Chief, then published poet, then temple Head Priest, then he took off his robes in nihilist despair. Then he became headmaster of a southern Island charity school, then prolific writer and drunk, then would-be suicide, then militant nationalist rebel against police state, then Secty. General of Association of Artists for Practical Freedom, then detainee & political jailbird, meanwhile prolific writer, translator and literary archivist, then at age 50 a husband and father, then epic-historical militant bard, prisoner in 1980, then epic poet of *Paekdu Mountain* and narrative poet of character vignettes *Ten Thousand Lives,* a monumental series of anecdotal "characters" written in Korean spoken idiom, finally a demon-driven Bodhisattva of Korean poetry, exuberant, demotic, abundant, obsessed with poetic creation, "Widely acknowledged to be Korea's foremost contemporary poet," according to his translators.

Familiar with some of his earlier poems in Translations[*], especially some of the later trickster-like naturalistic life sketches of *Ten Thousand Lives*— tender portraits, humane, paradoxical, "ordinary" stories with hilarious twists & endings, a little parallel to the "Characters" of W. C. Williams and Charles Reznikoff, I was stopped short by *Beyond Self: 108 Korean Zen Poems,* the present volume. 108 (count of beads in Buddhist mala) thought-stopping Koanlike mental firecrackers. I haven't gone thru Zen Practice, my lineage is Tibetan Kagyu, just sitting and Gelugpa, some analytical meditation. But everyone eastern-literate knows the taste of Koan & Haiku & gatha & doha nonconceptual riddles—or conceptions that annul Conceptual speculation.

Ko Un backtracks from earlier "Crazy Wisdom" narratives & here presents what I take to be Zen minipoems. I can't account for them, only half understand their implications and am attracted by the nubbin of poetry they present. Hard nuts to crack—yet many seem immediately nutty & empty at the same time: "before your mom / your burbling / was there" i.e. Chortling you had before you were born.

Reminiscent of Ikkyu's manifestation of shunyata, "Oh yes things exist, like the echo of your voice when you yell at the foot of a huge mountain" (Steven Berg. Tr.), Ko Un notices while *Walking down a mountain,* "The autumn breeze tosses and turns lifeless / like a cast-off snake skin."

The luminous broad humor's apparent: *A drunk-ard* "...staggering zigzag along. / Sixty trillion cells! All drunk!"

Ko Un's imagination roves *In a cramped prison cell,* "Italy today / Spain tomorrow / travel around a bit / Sri Lanka the day after."

And we have Classic ordinary mind (& speech & body): "Look, if you've had your shit, / wipe yourself and get out of here."

Or on Samsara, a *Mosquito:* "Why, I'm really alive. / Scratch scratch."

A little Blakean empathy: "The worm dribbled a cry."

And a sense of quick transience: "That dog that'll die tomorrow/ doesn't know it's going to die / It's barking fiercely."

Ko Un is a magnificent poet, combination of Buddhist cognoscente, passionate political libertarian, and naturalist historian. This little book of Son (Zen) poems gives a glimpse of the severe humorous discipline beneath the prolific variety of his forms & subjects. These excellent translations are models useful to inspire American Contemplative poets.

Allen Ginsberg
August 27, 1994
Elmwood Park, NJ

---

* *The Sound of My Waves: Selected Poems by Ko Un,* translated by Brother Anthony of Taizé and Young-Moo Kim (Ithaca, NY: Cornell East Asia Series, 1993).

Foreword
by Thich Nhat Hanh

In 1995, the poet Ko Un interviewed me for a program on the Buddhist television network in Seoul. As we sat together in the studio, sharing our thoughts and experiences on many topics, I felt I was in the presence of a Dharma brother. I told him I had the feeling we had done this many times before. The more I learned about his life, the closer I felt to him. Ko Un was a Buddhist monk, and he is also a poet, a writer, and an ardent worker for peace. He is also a man of great insight. When he was imprisoned by the military dictatorship for his efforts for peace, his deep Buddhist practice sustained him. Living mindfully in each moment, he knew what to do and what not to do to help himself and others as well.

When I was staying in the hills above Seoul, I was deeply moved by the spring magnolia flowers just outside my door. I entered the present moment deeply, and I said to them, "Magnolia flowers, I *know* you are there, and that makes me very happy." I hope you will enjoy these poems in the same way. As you read Ko Un's poems, allow the poet in you to hear his voice.

His poems are vivid, imaginative, and filled with light. Enter deeply into the present moment, reflect on each word, and meet the poet Ko Un face to face.

Thich Nhat Hanh
Plum Village, France
July 1997

Introduction
Ko Un: A Traveler on the Way
by Ok-Koo Kang Grosjean

"I did not come to this world to play. As birds sing, I came to this world to sing, keep silent, and to work." —Ko Un

Ko Un was born August 1, 1933, the first son of a farmer in a small village in North Cholla Province. He was a sickly infant, and at times it seemed doubtful whether he would survive. But he did. As a young boy, he studied Chinese classics and learned to read and write Korean from a neighbor's servant. (Under Japanese colonialism, it was prohibited to teach Korean in schools.) He entered primary school at age ten, and when Korea was liberated from Japanese rule, he was the only student in his class who knew how to read and write Korean. Ko Un was also talented in painting. One day he placed a note on his wall that said, "There is no one but van Gogh." It was his dream to become a painter.

In 1949, a year before the Korean War, Ko Un found a book of poems along the roadside by Han

Ha-Wun, the beloved Korean leper-poet. He spent the whole night reading and weeping. Han Ha-Wun had deeply affected him, and he decided to become a poet. He wandered the streets doing whatever work he could to make a living, and finally he was hired to teach Korean and art.

The 1950–1953 war had a deep effect on Ko Un. He witnessed unspeakable violence by the Communists—rape, murder, suicide, brothers killing brothers. When the Korean army regained the country, they killed anyone who had participated in the Communist regime, including Ko Un's family members, neighbors, friends, relatives, and his first love. Ko Un was given the order to transport corpses, and he carried them on his back for many nights. Overwhelmed by the suffering, Ko Un roamed the hills and mountains, and many thought he had gone insane. He finally quit his job as a teacher and began working as a clerk for the American Navy. It was during that time that he heard about the monk Hyech'o and determined to meet him.

Hyech'o was the son of Park Je-Sun, one of the five officials who turned Korea over to Japan at the end of the Yi Dynasty. Hyech'o's shame at this drove him to become a monk. In 1952, at age nineteen, Ko Un became a novice monk under Hyech'o's guidance. He was given the Buddhist name Chungchang and the *kongan*,[1] "All the dharmas return to the one. Where does the one return?" But within a year Hyech'o fell in love and left the monkhood. Ko Un's shock was so great he attempted suicide.

Ko Un wandered as a begging monk for a year. Finally, exhausted, he went to see Master Hyobong, and received the kongan *Mu* (literally: "No," "Nothingness," "Emptiness"). Ko Un described his new master as "very kind and very strict." Hyobong Sonsa had previously been a lawyer and judge. Once he had to demand the death penalty, and he was so tormented that he left his family and became a disciple of Sokdu Sonsa.[2] When Hyobong arrived, Sokdu Sonsa asked him, "How many steps did you take to come here?" Hyobong circled the room, and Sokdu accepted him as his disciple.

One day, while washing rice in the monastery, Ko Un dropped a few grains. Hyobong Sonsa saw this and started crying at the waste of this precious food. Ko Un had the realization that the spiritual and material are one from the very beginning. After that day, Ko Un never wasted one grain of rice. He even gathered rice that been thrown into the ditch as refuse. Ko Un recollects, "Before I became a disciple of Hyobong Sonsa, I was very knowledgeable about Western philosophy, sutra study, and the teachings of the early Son[3] Patriarchs. In fact, I was pedantic and enjoyed showing off. Seeing this, my master said, 'Be ignorant in everything. Let go of everything and only meditate on "Mu." Mu is your breath, your farts, and your father. Let go even of emptiness.' Free from

words, I began to fly, and from this freedom, I met
with language again."

Korea is a land of poetry. While young people in the
West dream of being movie stars or athletes, Korean
young people dream of becoming poets. Everyone,
regardless of status, throughout Korean history has
written poetry. Poetry and poets are revered in Korea
and Ko Un aspired to be a poet. When he became
editor of *The Buddhist Newspaper,* he wrote poems
to fill all the empty spaces.

During the Japanese occupation, the quality of
monks and nuns in Korea had declined, and Ko Un
did his best to try to restore the Sangha, train monks,
and educate laypeople. Ko Un practiced meditation
traditionally, but he was also wild. One rainy day, he
danced naked on the grounds of the Chogye Temple,
and the other monks followed his example! Then while
studying Ashvaghosa's *The Awakening of Faith in the
Mahayana,* Ko Un had a realization—that emptiness
is not nihilistic, that to understand emptiness is to
realize the oneness of all beings. This was a turning
point in his life.

In 1959, Ko Un entered the beautiful Haein-sa,
one of the three main Buddhist monasteries in Korea.
One day while walking beside a stream, he found a

human skull. He took it to his room and every night he talked to the skull:

Did you practice hard?
No, I wasted the whole day.
Ah, that's the problem.
What's the problem?
That you pretend to practice.
Oh, you skull Zen master!
Oh, you future skull Zen master!

In 1960, when Syngman Rhee's government was overthrown, Ko Un was at Haein-sa. The Rhee government had supported monks who were celibate, and now, the formerly excluded married monks[4] gathered force and attempted to gain temples they had lost under the Rhee administration. One day Ko Un was notified that some monks were approaching Haein-sa, accompanied by thugs. Everyone left the temple except Ko Un and a few young monks. Ko Un said, "It was not that I had courage, but I had to stay. We began to meditate. I wore the official robe and held the temple seal in my hand. When the married monks came, they couldn't do anything. Our meditation posture kept them from taking any action. But in the afternoon, they got the thugs drunk, and the gang members dragged me down by my arms and legs, tearing my robe and scraping my head on the stone steps. The monks asked me to transfer Haein-sa to them, and I shouted, 'Kill me now.'" Praised for saving Haein-sa, Ko Un was given the position of abbot. However, within a short time, he resigned, buried the skull, and accepted an abbotship at Jondung-sa on Kanghwa Island. There, he thought deeply about his future as a monk and poet.

In 1963, he published an essay announcing his return to secular life. He feared that if he tried to master both Son and poetry at the same time he would lose both. So he chose one—literature. But the secular world did not receive Ko Un kindly.

He spent some of his time browsing in secondhand bookstores. In one store, he found a Japanese translation of Mikhail Sholokhov's novel, *And Quiet Flows the Don,* recounting the struggles of individuals living in the midst of the Russian Revolution. Ko Un read the book every night for seven days, deeply moved by its grief and suffering. The book led him to disparage his own work along with all of Korea's literary output for the previous half century. One night, he drank four bottles of liquor, collected all his works, and burned them. He felt it was not literature, compared with the work of Sholokhov.

After another failed suicide attempt, Ko Un lived on Cheju Island for four years, established a library and a public high school, and taught Korean and art to poor children. However, he continued to drink heavily and he suffered from insomnia. When he returned to Seoul, his insomnia continued, and he was tormented by a nihilism that affected many intellectuals after the Korean War. In 1970, Ko Un made his last suicide attempt. He was discovered by army reservists in a valley near Seoul and recovered consciousness after thirty hours. It was the beginning of a new life as an activist. During this period, Ko Un published many books of poetry and essays.

In the winter of 1970, Ko Un was spending the night at a tavern, and found an old newspaper on the floor with an article about a laborer's self-immolation. Why did this young man have to die, while I am still alive? he thought. The article pulled Ko Un out of the abyss and changed his life forever.

In the 1970s and 1980s, Ko Un was a leading political activist, protesting Korea's military dictatorship. He participated in the labor and unification movements and was regularly visited by the Korean CIA, and followed by policemen wherever he went. He was tortured, and, as a result, lost his hearing. He now has an artificial eardrum. In 1980 he was imprisoned, together with many others, at the time of the tragic events known as the Kwangju Democratic Uprising, in which so many innocent lives were lost.[5] Ko Un was falsely accused of conspiring to incite civil war. In his dark cell, he realized the interconnectedness of all beings, and he resolved to create something to commemorate all the people he had known from Korean history and during his life. In 1982, aged forty-nine, he was released by a special pardon. The following year he married Lee Sang-Hwa, a professor of English literature. In 1985, their daughter, Cha-Ryong, was born.

"I was born because of literature, and because of literature I have a life that should have ended many times. Eventually my death will be literature itself. Literature has to reveal the highest truth and challenge all lies. I can only write in my native language. Even my prepositions are bloodstained blossoms that contain the life and history of all my ancestors." Many of Ko Un's literary works—more than one hundred volumes of poems, essays, critical reviews, and novels—spring from his practice of Zen. They either minimize language or free themselves from language. When Ko Un left the monastery, he left behind corrupt organization, not Buddhism. His Zen Buddhism is always with him. He has said that, while in prison, it was Zen that sustained him.

Ko Un published his first book of poetry, *Other World Sensitivity*, in 1960, just after the April revolution that overthrew the Rhee government. From 1960 to 1967, Ko Un wrote mostly lyric poems, often focusing on death. From 1974 to 1983, he wrote passionate, untamed political poems. Since 1984, beginning with the publication of *Homeland Stars*, he has entered a new phase of affirmation. His present work in process, conceived in prison, is *Ten Thousand Lives,* commemorating both historical and obscure personages. So far, fifteen volumes have been published.

In 1991, Ko Un completed a best-selling Buddhist novel *Hwaom-kyong (Garland Sutra),* based on *The Avatamsaka Sutra,* describing Sudhana's endless quest for truth.

In Ko Un's early work, he sees emptiness without form; in his middle period as a passionate political activist, he sees form; in his later years, after the experience of solitary confinement and of being a husband and father, he sees form in emptiness and emptiness in form.

His current work focuses on themes of self and no-self, based on the teachings of Buddhism and the work of Lao Tzu and Chuang Tzu. He uses both Zen-like direct language and a vast epic style. He has recently published *Son,* a novel in two volumes about important Zen masters since Bodhidharma, and an epic poem in seven volumes, *Paekdu-san,* describing the independence movement during the Japanese occupation of Korea.

What are Zen poems? You have to taste each poem. That is their beauty. Ko Un asks us to participate in the festivity of our lives and to move beyond our usual limits. That is one reason Zen masters sometimes use irreverent language to shock us beyond our usual restrictions.

It is my great joy to introduce Ko Un, a truly compassionate poet, who said, "One must cry many days before becoming a poet." These 108 Son poems are not only 108 glimpses of Ko Un. They are also 108 chances to look at ourselves.

Ok-Koo Kang Grosjean
Albany, California
June 1997

[1] A meditation topic. Similar to Japanese koan.

[2] Sokdu Sonsa was a Korean Son master who practiced in the Diamond Mountains and was Hyobong Sonsa's teacher. He was known as a master who did not accept students freely.

[3] Son is the Korean pronunciation of Dhyana, which means meditation, and is commonly known in English by its Japanese transliteration "Zen."

[4] Traditionally, Buddhist monks are celibate. The Japanese changed that tradition in the 19th Century, and during their occupation of Korea, imposed marriage on Korean Buddhist monks.

[5] Military leader Chun Doo-Hwan had massacred many citizens of Kwangju, who had tried to begin a new era of democracy after the assassination of military dictator Park Chung-Hee.

Reference
Buswell, Jr., Robert E. 1992. *The Zen Monastic Experience: Buddhist Practice in Contemporary Korea.* Princeton: Princeton University Press.

Poet's Preface
by Ko Un

The whole world renewed! I want to offer water to all who thirst for a new world. I want to light a fire so they can warm themselves on a cold evening.

I long to give them bars of iron to hold on to, to prevent them from being swept away by raging storms. But people made of mud cannot cross streams, people made of wood cannot go near a fire. And people made of iron will rust away in less than a century.

Here stands a good-for-nothing who let himself get soaked till the mud dissolved, set fire to himself so the wood disappeared, and whose iron finally rusted away in the wind and the rain. Go now. The new world is found wherever new life comes to birth.

The Buddhist meditative tradition is called Son[*] in Korean, Zen in Japanese, Ch'an in Chinese, Dhyana in Sanskrit. Son comes alive by first denying speech and writing.

That makes it an incomparably thrilling exercise. This denial is a realistic reflection of the practice of Son. Initially the practice of Son entered China and took root in the philosophies of Lao Tzu and Chuang Tzu, yet this early Chinese Buddhism prematurely hardened into a grand metaphysics of the upper classes. It was perfectly adapted to function as an elite form of speech and writing.

Son offered the means by which the importance attached to the acts of speaking and writing could be overthrown in a powerful grassroots movement of rejection.

As a result, Son obliged those who knew how to write to reject writing completely, and became accessible to people who could not utter a single word.

Moreover, Son contributed to the legitimization of the role of the ordinary common people and even of slaves, by rejecting the religious system centered on the monastic life. The Third Patriarch, Seng Ts'an, and the Sixth, Hui Neng, were active in this direction.

Son is mind and nothing else. Only through the true character within the mind can a radically new world, one totally different from the old, be experienced; that is the goal of Son.

Son sets out to come to the truth of all things by the rejection of all things and yet, despite this negative approach, the free dialogue of Son's famous questions and answers was able to arise, as well as Son poetry. By the eighth century Son had already given rise to the first age of Son literature.

Son literature is an intense act of the mind liberated from the established systems of speech and writing, a new and completely unfamiliar system. It is the vitality arising from this unfamiliarity that lies at the heart of Son poetry.

This vitality underlies the fascinating tensions, the urgency, and the outrageous ellipses that strongly characterize Son poems, and even works not usually so termed, to the point that perhaps all poems are really in the end Son poems!

Buddhist canonical writings can be classified into roughly twelve categories according to their literary types. Among them we find *Gatha,* which are essentially poetic works, and *Gayya,* where something that has first been expressed in prose is given added force by the use of verse. Here we may find the origins of Son poetry.

Son poetry enjoyed its initial Golden Age high in the mountains of T'ang China (618–907) and its history has continued down the centuries until the present day, spanning more than a thousand years.

Son has preserved its own characteristics, so that while Son and poetry go together, there is no instance of its ever having integrated the tedious narratives and descriptions found in other forms of literature. Which explains why Zen masters are poets, never novelists.

Through ten years' experience of Son life as a monk I gained some experience of Son poetry. As for the power of literature, which lies on the opposite side from that experience, it has reconciled me to the fact that although Son may reject the act of writing I am free to incorporate its substance as a proper subject for literature. That has been my assurance throughout my thirty-five years as a poet.

Consequently, this collection of Son poems is an act of poetry but at the same time it is an act of Son, and therefore not so much intent on being faithful to the history of Son poetry as determined to get free from it.

I too need to encounter water, fire, iron, because my ceaseless dream and desire is for a new world. Surely Son is nothing other than a love for that world, just as a mother always knows what her kids are up to, and kids are always looking for their mother.

Ko Un
Ansong, Korea

·

° The "o" in Son is pronounced as in "on," not as in "sun."

ECHO

To mountains at dusk:
What are you?

What are you are you...

THE OWL

Midday owl
eyes squinting
I can't see a thing.
Just wait.
Your night's sure to come.

BABY

Before you were born
before your dad
before your mom

your burbling
               was there.

BLIND ANIRUDDHA

This man sank so deep into meditation
he lost his sight for good
but heaven's eyes have opened.
He sees all that exists.

WALKING DOWN A MOUNTAIN

Looking back
      Hey!
Where's the mountain I've just come down?
Where am I?
The autumn breeze tosses and turns lifeless
      like a cast-off snakeskin.

BEEF

Everything turning into something.
The most disheartening of moments.
      Cut it off

Everything turning into something
while cows are turning into beef.

THREE NAMES

They're playing with Zen like children.
It's white! It's black! Quarrels too.
Let's call it quits.
Then
get up dusting each other off.

Once
for no reason
Chusa gave Baekpa
three separate names and said
If eligible people appear
       later
allocate one of these to each of them
       Sokjon
       Manam
       Daryun
Sokjon went to the obscure Park Han-Yong
Manam to Song Jong-Hon
and then came the monk Daryun.

One name
Manam
now hangs framed in Paekyang Temple
where at midnight the night bird sings.

BUSHMEN

For African bushmen
a dozen words are enough
for a whole lifetime

Oh true Father Son and Holy Spirit. Bushmen.

FATHOMING

Come here.

No feet.

I'm sending a bitch
to bite your feet.

You son of a bitch!

Come tomorrow.

Tomorrow? What's tomorrow?

You son of a bitch!

BEYOND

Without you
how can I possibly live?

MEMORIES

Waiting decades for one snowflake
my body of charcoal has glowed
glowed and gone out.

The cicadas have stopped singing.

THE MONK KYONGHO

You wouldn't be you
would you
if you didn't know all about wine and women?
Only you didn't know about the rest
so look
                   a couple of magpies
have built their nest in your hair.

BROAD DAYLIGHT

A dry turd
with no flies around.

Is this Paradise? No.

A SMILE

Standing in front of the smile
on the face of a boiled pig's head

by all means be as generous.

CLOTHES

King Ashoka brought a suit of clothes
Manjushri hid away.
No help for it
King Ashoka went back home
and put the suit on.
Then he saw that "river is river."

A DRUNKARD

I've never been an individual entity.
Sixty trillion cells!
I'm a living collection
staggering zigzag along.
Sixty trillion cells! All drunk.

THE LOTUS SUTRA

The Lotus Sutra. Ultimate reality.
So far
you've been bashing me badly.
Now
I'll cudgel you, bastard.
Oh! Ouch!
Take that too.
Oh! Ouch!
Oh! Ouch!

The Lotus Sutra dashed away.
       Fields open wide, once the farmers
have gone.

SITTING

If you sit Buddha dies mother dies.
Don't sit.
Don't stand.
All five oceans six continents
       even
that cinnamon tree in the bright moonlight
here and there are all a boiling cauldron
with nowhere to put your feet down.
What's to be done?

AN ALLEY

A blind alley. I turn back.
       Great.
Here and there
bright lights

Up an alley in hill-girt Chongnung.

MOON AND MIDDAY

Sun-face Buddha has lived eighteen hundred
years
Moon-face Buddha has lived one single night
Sun-face Moon-face are not two but one.
If that's true
moonrise comes
after sunset.

What about that daytime moon up there?
Sheer ignorance!

A TEMPLE'S MAIN HALL

A big mistake!

Much better
to have turned back at the front gate.

THE MASTER'S SCROLL

The monk Ta Hui of ancient Sung
set fire to his master's scroll
              of the Blue Cliff Records.
Well done. He did well.

Yet here's the work in question.

A RAINBOW

There are such things, straightening clothes.

SOUTH AND NORTH

The head monk of Bohyon Temple
up in Myohyang Mountain dialed
and the head monk of Taehung Temple
down in Haenam took the call.
How are you getting on these days?
Our Buddha's turned round.
Ours has turned round too.

Not only there.
North and South, every Buddha had turned
round.

What fine fellows.

SON ROOM

Try sitting
      not just for one kalpa
but for ten kalpas.
No enlightenment will come.

Simply play for a while with troubles, illusions,
      then stand up.

LATE SUMMER

Into water. Splash!
Into flames.
Eek, hot!

I go bouncing on like this
      while berries ripen beyond.

A SUDDEN SHOWER

Several billion Buddhas pouring down.
The brook busy babbling.
In addition
to the Buddha corpses
other corpses are floating down too.
Real cool.

IDLE TALK

Dharma's father was Hui K'o.
Shen Hsiu and Hui Neng were Hung Jen's
fathers.
Shen Hsiu had fun in the palace.
Hui Neng had so many fathers
that the southern rivers and lakes got dizzy.

A really immoral family!

A FRIEND

Hey! With the clay you dug out
I fashioned a Buddha.
It rained.
The Buddha turned back into clay.

Clear skies after rain are pointless.

GLEANING

A patriarch's sayings are
ears of grain in a field
this year of poor harvests.
With them…

CROSSROADS INN

Awake?
If awake joy
sorrow nowhere.
As I looked out after three bowls of wine
at a crossroads inn,
that's what I heard the rain-swept road say.

DAYFLY

Three hundred-millionths of a second.
If that's how long one particle lasts
think how endless one day is.
You think a day's too short?
Greedy thing.

A PHANTOM

The deer have grown really long horns.
Now the autumn breeze
                                    has got caught on their
horns
and can't budge an inch.

What's that passing over the hill? Hey you!

A ROSARY

Angulimala was a devil of a cutthroat.
That fellow
sliced off the fingers of the people he killed
and wore them
strung dingle-dangle around his neck
his father's finger too.

That was a real hundred-eight bead rosary.
Every bead on the string
a life.

THE MOON

The bow taut.
Twang!
The arrow strikes

                      your eye.

By the pain of your darkness the moon rose.

ONE WORD

Too quick! Too quick!
Call a stick of firewood
fire. Oh dear.

LEPERS

Nonsense is not eighty-four thousand.
Oh! sounds
Gosh! sounds
all nonsense.
Pull out Bodhidharma's eyebrows.
Pull out the Sixth Patriarch's toenails.

Ah, some lepers are playing their pipes over
there.

MASTER POJO OF KORYO

One fellow stood on his head
did yoga till he died.
Another one
piled up wood that he set alight
then climbed on top
a "Lotus in Flames."

Master Pojo of Koryo
took his place on the podium
answered all the Hundred Questions
then got down from the podium
and sat on the edge of the porch…

Green leaves turn red then die.
Oh no that won't do.

A GREEN FROG

One green frog.
Black clouds are filling the sky.
Just because you croaked.

What a Hercules.
You squirt.

IN YOUR BOSOM

A century in your bosom.
No nation
No friends
No way for me to take.

What rapture, the ground of darkness.

CUCKOO

At dawn three cuckoos sit side by side.
Not a word about
How fine this world!
How fine that world!
Yesterday's cuckoo-cuckoo quite forgotten.
Too early yet for today's cuckoo-cuckoo.
The best time of day!

A SMILE

Shakyamuni held up a lotus
so Kashyapa smiled.
Not at all.
The lotus smiled
so Kashyapa smiled.

Nowhere was Shakyamuni!

THE HORIZON

I stood facing the horizon over the East Sea.
What had become of the seventeen hundred
koan-riddles?
  The sound of waves
  the sound of waves.
Playing with you I threw them away.

MOUNTAIN IS MOUNTAIN

"Mountain is mountain
water is water," Tai Neng chanted.
"Mountain is not mountain
water is not water," Tai Neng chanted.
Eat your food.
Once you've eaten, go shit.

MOUNTAINTOP

What do you think there is up on the mountaintop?
Come down.
A peach tree's flowering at the crossroads.
"I'm off again today…"

FARAWAY LIGHTS

Traveling by night
distant lights were my strength.
By them alone
by them alone
yesterday today and tomorrow too.

RIPPLES

Look! Do all the ripples move
because one ripple starts to move?
      No.
It's just that all the ripples move at once.

Everything's been askew from the start.

BABY MAGPIES

You idiot. Don't you know?
Shakyamuni's dad wasn't King Suddhodana.
            He was a demon.

Clumsy chatter of baby magpies at dawn. How
cute.

ASKING THE WAY

You blockheads who ask what Buddha is
should start asking about every sentient being
instead.
Ask about everything.
When you're hungry
            ask about food.
Ask the moonlight about the way.
Find a port where lemon trees bloom
            where lemon trees bloom.
Ask about places to drink in the port.

Ask and ask till nothing's left to ask.

BLUE SKIES

Hey, man, cry your eyes out.

IN A CRAMPED PRISON CELL

If all the nations aren't in here
where are the fine
fluttering flags of every country?
Italy today
Spain tomorrow
          travel around a bit
Sri Lanka the day after.

A LION

The lion's in the cave!
          Lurks
The lion's out of the cave!
          Looks
The lion's at the edge of the cave!
          Looms
The lion's run away!
          Limps

Is this kind of stuff a proper job for a grasshopper?

THE PATH

Take this path. It leads to Nirvana.

Excuse me.
I'll go where I want to.
Over rocky crags or under water.

The Master's path is the corpse's path.

A KIND OF CATASTROPHE

One kind of bird eats up its mother.

The mother hatching and feeding her chick
is feeding her own death.
Like mother like chick.
Eating up mother
is the natural thing for mother and chick.

THE WASH

The wash flaps, a bodhisattva not knowing it's a
bodhisattva.

PALGONG MOUNTAIN

Jails are crammed full of great masters.
Killer-and-thief, thief-and-killer,
would be killer-thief and all the rest.

Taegu jail here is crammed full
but in every temple on Palgong Mountain
without any great masters
not even a great master's cousin
wind bells tinkle.

THE WIND

Never beg the wind for mercy.
Tall wild lilies and such
scented white lilies and such
one-day lilies and such
once all your stems have snapped
produce new buds. It's not too late.

ONE DAY

Lightning over the hill in front
thunder on the hill behind
between the two
        one dumb pebble.

SIMPLY

We say we're taking
the way we're each taking
because someone else told us to take it.
We say the water simply flowing down the hills
      is flowing
because someone told it to.
Human wisdom's wretched stuff.

STEAK

Drinking in downtown Taejon
my mouth was stuffed full
with a big lump of broiled steak
but suddenly I couldn't swallow it
      couldn't spit it out...
outside the pouring rain was shouting:
Quick! Say something!

What?

IN DAYLIGHT

After the rain, with water everywhere.
Twelve no thirfourfifsixteen swallows soaring
high.

BELL STREET

I went strolling down Bell Street in Taegu
          then drank a bottle of schnapps I'd
bought.

OLD BUDDHA

Hey, were you talking about old Buddha?
Why, old Buddha's no Buddha.
Real Buddha's a fish just netted
          leaping and jumping.

A STONE IN A RIDGE BETWEEN TWO FIELDS

Aha, real Buddha's out of doors.
The future world?
It's opening like this
          partly inside partly out.

And all the long long day
          cuckoos chant prayers.

REEDS IN CHEJU ISLAND

Early November. Cheju reed fields
white with tufted reeds
a scarecrow in the middle.

It's watching the sea. The sea's watching it.

MOON

What's that? We only have to look at the moon?
Forget about "the finger pointing at the moon?"
          You blockhead!

Who cares if you forget moon and finger?

ODAE MOUNTAIN

Mount Odae clapped
so Mount Ami laughed.

Where's that, Mount Ami?
At the end of half-a-day's nap.

SPRING DREAMS

The night before last I beat up Han Shan in a
dream.
Last night I held Chunhyang in a dream.
Yesterday I received twenty phone calls.
Today I bought ten strong nails
after walking out of a Chinese movie
       at Kwangshin Cinema in Ansong.
Back home I hammered in the nails and hung
up photos.

Perfect! Han Shan and Chunhyang in photos.

A GREEN FROG

My master is not Hyobong the monk.
Stirring ever so slightly
stuck at the end of a pole
for ten years now it's been a green frog.

RIPPLES

Stoop lower and lower
till you're nearly not quite touching the ripples.

There's the bodhisattva Manjushri.

HEAVY RAIN

Rain pouring down all day long
not a beast left in sight.
Alright!
You guys! Come out!
        Come out and play in the rain.

You must. The day after tomorrow it's the sky's
turn.

WEAKLINGS

If there are great men
interestingly enough
there are weaklings too.
Who are they?
Fellows lacking an ordinary heart.

The monk Nan Ch'uan used to go on about
how the ordinary heart really is the Tao.

WIND

A wind stirs.
Ah, this world that world.

LEAVING HOME

If going away is what it is to be a monk
then coming back
      really
      really
is what it is to be a Buddha.

But surely you can only really come back
               if you've really gone away?

THE HERMIT

Jang Ku-Song the hermit was busy shitting
when he heard frogs croaking. It made him
recite

The croaking of frogs on moonlit nights in early
spring
pierces the world from end to end, makes us all
one family.

Look, if you've had your shit,
          wipe yourself and get out of here.

WORDS I LIKE

I'd rather sink to the bottom of the sea
        till the end of time
than get liberation with the help of a lot of
sages. Great! I've got wine in my glass
        and this saying of Master Stonehead's
too.

MOSQUITO

I've been bitten by a mosquito.
Thanks a million.
Why, I'm really alive.
        Scratch scratch.

HAN SHAN AND SHIH TE

Don't go serving those fools
        Han Shan and Shih Te
like so many people do.
Today I plan to run to T'ien-T'ai Mountain,
pull it all down and
plant opium poppies where it stood.
Yes, red opium poppies.

THE WOMEN OF MAJONG

The women of Majong village
the old women
once all the girls had left the place
those old women
would help each other
in furrowed fields under a scorching sun.
Out weeding they'd stop work
to dance a merry dance
singing "Come back to Pusan harbor"
dancing a merry dance.

A NEW WAY

Sink into the sea.
Look how many companions you've got!
From whales and sharks right down to shrimps
all the way down to the darkest deep.

Don't go treading in Buddha's footsteps
            none of that stuff
just sink into the sea.

HOUSE

If it's very high the devil can't find it.
If it's very low Buddha can't find it.
Living in a house built there
gourd creepers climb with flowers dazzling at mid-
night.

A SINGLE WORD

Too late.

The world had already heard
      my word
before I spoke it.
The worm had heard.
The worm dribbled a cry.

SUMMER

The sightless sunflower follows the sun.
The sightless moonflower blossoms in moonlight.
      Foolishness.
That's all they know.
Dragonflies fly by day
      beetles by night.

A SHOOTING STAR

Wow! You recognized me.

AN AUTUMN NIGHT

Daddy
Daddy

A cricket sings.

TODAY

Haha! Today's the best day. The best
for some guy to kick the bucket
and for some other guy to get born
and start life whimpering whimpering.

The sky looks ominous.

EARTHWORM

The earthworm wriggles onwards.
Wriggles on then rests.
The sky's best friend.

A BOWL OF ROWAN TEA

Here's a bowl of rowan tea. Drink up.
Rather than sing praises of thousands of miles
        travel one or two.

Hey, you tongues.

ONE LITTLE KID

I refuse to seek refuge in the Three Jewels.
As I was walking along
I met one little kid
got fascinated by its innocence.
How useless are candles and things
       incense and things.
Oh dear! the dragonfly's got away.

SLAMMING THE DOOR

Go away. I'm not in.
Go and look
at the bottom of the sea.
Here's only a stray dog that shits
       then licks its dirt.

Yeuh!

FRIENDS

Hello there!
the shout rang out.
Cape Kuryong here!
Over the sea Ullong Island rejoined.
What's up?
Come across for a while.
Sure, I'll be right over.

The night waves were roaring
the lamplight was bright in one pub on Cape
Kuryong.

LATE ONE NIGHT

Late one night a fox changes its shape
and slips into your room as a pretty girl:
>   what will you do?

Don't be stupid. I'll grab her.

Haha, you fox's husband, you.
A fox is more fun than Buddha, of course.

>   You bet.

WHY KILL?

Let be. Please, let be.
Kill Buddha
if you meet him?
Kill mother and father
if you meet them? Why kill?
Things made of clay all fall to bits
once soaked by monsoon rains.

BIRTHPLACE

Don't ask Chunsong the monk about his Master
Han Yong-Un also known as Manhae.
       Never heard of him.
Don't ask Chunsong the monk where he came
from.
If he's asked where he was born
he says
       My mother's c-nt

A ceremonial robe draped
over his naked body
he sat in meditation.
Under this belly
that's my mother's son's pr-ck.

Even Greece and Rome find it funny.

A MOONLIT NIGHT

Everything's out here shining, bright.
The mortar's empty.

No wonder the grasshoppers are making a
racket.

A MOONLESS NIGHT

No moon up
yet the two hundred miles
between you and me
shine bright all the night long.
That dog that'll die tomorrow
            doesn't know it's going to die.
It's barking fiercely.

A NAP

All the world lies in the womb.
That was a good sleep.
How about going out somewhere

to mewl. That's all.

ONE FLY

The fly settled.
I squashed it with my palm.
      No more fly.
What's going on here?
You've got to be kidding.
What's going on here?

WILD BOARS

A group of wild boars
dug into the Golden Mountain.
As they dug deeper
the gold became more dazzling.

My deepest respects, master boars.

HARSH TRAINING

My, you're cooking a meal of sand!
Who's going to eat that?

Out in the fields the cereals are ripe.

Why, even the sparrows do better than you!
Ugh! Ouch!

THE POLE STAR

If you were to vanish
the north would vanish
the south would vanish
east and west would vanish.
            No.

TRIPITAKA KOREANA

Finding the way blocked by utter gibberish
I turned back
and saw
a snake.

Snakes know the ways of snakes so well.

ANANDA

Even Shakyamuni could never tame Ananda
but Kashyapa kicked him out and tamed him.
Throw away all you know.
Throw away all you don't know.
Then and only then one star shines bright.

RECORDS OF THE TRANSMISSION OF THE LAMP

Why do they keep the transmission secret?
Sons of bitches!
Bow-wow-wow!

On moonlit nights everything's out in the open.

A LETTER

Zen Master Hanam's reply
to a letter from Son Master Kyongbong

was one blank sheet of paper.

Ha-ha, they're only cousins not uncles.

YEH FU

Old Yeh Fu took his shit
smeared it on the walls of his cell.
Monks burned up Yeh Fu's Song in the Diamond
Sutra
claiming he was senile.

This tale's one part of Yeh Fu's Song...
Look closely look.

PIG

Before you no bandit called Shakyamuni
behind you no beggar called Maitreya

your snout's ready to grunt.

PARTING

Farewell.
Fare   well.

Translators' Note
by Young-Moo Kim and
Brother Anthony, of Taizé

There can be no more daunting task for a translator than to have to render the laconic but deeply-rooted spontaneity of poems such as those contained in this volume. Even more than usual, we realize that "poetry is what gets lost in translation" and cannot help recalling Ko Un's assertion (quoted in the Introduction) that his literature is only possible in his native language.

In some sense, of course, every poem is only fully "possible" in its native language. In saying that, Ko Un was reminding us that he writes in Korean for Koreans, and that he considers his writing to be inseparable from the agonizing processes of Korean history past, present, and future. Even poems as seemingly "unpolitical" as those in this volume are expressions of his vocation to be devoted to the making of a new, truly Korean culture in a reunified and fully independent land.

There are 108 poems in this collection, just as there are 108 beads on the Buddhist "rosaries" used in repetitive prayer, as well as 108 "karmic bonds" of passions and delusions. Some readers will be puzzled that we use the word "Son" where English-language Buddhism normally uses the Japanese word "Zen." The word in question was originally a Sanskrit term, *dhyana,* meaning "meditation," and when Buddhism came to China, the word came with it, represented by an ideogram that the Chinese pronounce "ch'an," the Vietnamese "thien," the Koreans "son," and the Japanese "zen." In view of the long centuries of suffering inflicted by Japan on Korea, it did not seem right to use the Japanese form in our translation.

It might be good if this little book helped remind the world that the Buddhist tradition of dhyana is not originally or exclusively Japanese, and that in Korea today there are many hundreds of celibate monks and nuns who sit all day long for years on end in meditation rooms hidden deep in the hills, a practice also shared by devout laypeople.

There is an old tradition of Korean Son poetry which was often rather formal and philosophical. In modern times, some Korean poets have given the name to a style of spontaneous verse not unlike ink-paintings made by a single free movement of the brush after long concentration. Ko Un follows this pattern, but takes his poems even further toward the realities of daily life in today's Korea. These translations invite the reader to undertake multiple journeys in time, space, history, and culture, as well as within themselves.

We were deeply touched by Allen Ginsberg's response to our work and very much wish that he could have still been with us to see the poems published.

Young-Moo Kim
Brother Anthony, of Taizé
Seoul, Korea
May 1997

Notes

ECHO (PAGE 3)
The one-word question "Muonya? What are you? What's that?" is one of the fundamental challenges in the Korean Son tradition.

BLIND ANIRUDDHA (PAGE 4)
Aniruddha was a member of the family of Shakyamuni and a contemporary of the historical Buddha; there are tales of how he would always fall asleep while the Master taught but later studied deeply and so at last attained enlightenment.

THREE NAMES (PAGE 5)
Chusa was the pen name of Kim Jong-Hee (1786–1856), famous for his calligraphy. The other names are monks, of whom the "obscure" Park Han-Yong is the most famous since he was the friend of some of the greatest early modern Korean poets in the Independence Movement, and the teacher of the poet So Chong-Ju (Midang). Paekyang Temple is in South Cholla Province.

FATHOMING (PAGE 6)
The title of this poem is a word used in Son to designate a form of dialogue in which a master fathoms the extent to which a disciple has advanced in understanding.

THE MONK KYONGHO (PAGE 7)

Kyongho (1846–1912) entered a monastery when he was nine, began to study sutras at fourteen, and taught at twenty-three. When he was fifty-nine, he suddenly disappeared, then reappeared with a new name. He practiced a controversial Way which included breaking precepts.

CLOTHES (PAGE 8)

King Ashoka (ca. 264 B.C.E.– ca. 226 B.C.E.), having unified India, made Buddhism its official religion and launched a vast program of buildings for which he inaugurated Buddhist art. Manjushri is the name of the bodhisattva of wisdom and intellect. "River is river" is an echo of a famous Chinese Ch'an story about Tai Neng (see the poem "Mountain is mountain" on page 31).

THE LOTUS SUTRA (PAGE 9)

The *Lotus Sutra* is one of the most important works in the Buddhist canon but Son tends to deny the importance of written teachings in favor of direct personal experience.

SITTING (PAGE 9)

Sitting is the standard expression for "doing Son meditation" since it traditionally involves sitting for long periods of time. The challenge to "kill Buddha" and "kill parents" is part of the Buddhist search for detachment from all bonds.

AN ALLEY (PAGE 10)

Chongnung was until recently an isolated, hill-girt village to the north of Seoul.

THE MASTER'S SCROLL (PAGE 11)

The "Blue Cliff Records" were compiled between 1111 and 1117 by the Chinese Ch'an Master Yuan Wu K'o Ch'in.

SOUTH AND NORTH (PAGE 11)
Myohyang Mountain is in North Korea, Haenam is in the southernmost part of South Cholla Province; temples in the two places are made the setting for an evocation of the total division of the two parts of Korea, between which telephone conversations are not permitted. The statues have each turned to face the other half of Korea.

SON ROOM (PAGE 12)
A *kalpa* is the number of years it takes for heaven and Earth to pass through one complete cycle of abolition and renewal, the largest conceivable unit of time.

IDLE TALK (PAGE 13)
The names mentioned here are those of some of the Six Patriarchs, great masters of the Chinese Ch'an Schools; Bodhidharma was an Indian, the legendary First Patriarch, perhaps active in China between 470 and 570. Hui Neng (638–713) is the Sixth. In this poem the hierarchy of master and disciple is deliberately confused. The story of how Hung Jen, the Fifth Patriarch, chose the temple's kitchen-boy Hui Neng to be his successor rather than Shen Hsiu, who was its chief monk, is found in the "Liu Tsu T'an Ching," composed in about 820.

A ROSARY (PAGE 15)
Angulimala is reputed to have lived in the days of the historical Buddha. He was said to have killed over ninety people and to have promised that his hundredth victim would be his own mother.

LEPERS (PAGE 16)
On Bodhidharma see the note to "Idle Talk" above. In Chinese art, he is represented with eyebrows reaching to the ground.

MASTER POJO OF KORYO (PAGE 16)
Pojo is a name given posthumously to the Korean Son master Chinul, who founded Songkwang Temple in South Cholla Province.

A SMILE (PAGE 18)
A famous story tells how Shakyamuni silently held up a lotus flower; the other disciples were puzzled but (Maha-)Kashyapa smiled, showing that he had understood the implied wordless message. This is seen as the beginning of the Son tradition.

THE HORIZON (PAGE 18)
The kind of paradoxical riddle-question used in Son is usually called a koan in English, from the Japanese pronunciation of the Chinese characters.

MOUNTAIN IS MOUNTAIN (PAGE 18)
See note to "Clothes" (page 46).

BABY MAGPIES (PAGE 20)
King Suddhodana is the name given to the father of the historical Buddha Shakyamuni in the traditional tales.

PALGONG MOUNTAIN (PAGE 23)
Palgong Mountain is near Taegu, in the southeastern part of Korea.

MOON (PAGE 26)
When they want to distinguish between essence and means, Korean Masters often refer to a traditional saying: "The finger pointing at the moon is not the moon."

SPRING DREAMS (PAGE 27)
Han Shan was a famous monk poet of ancient China, also known in English by the translation of his name, Cold Mountain.

Chunhyang is the heroine of Korea's most popular ancient love story.

WEAKLINGS (PAGE 28)
Nan Ch'uan (748–834) was a Chinese monk.

WORDS I LIKE (PAGE 30)
The name "Master Stonehead" is quite common among Son monks in both China and Korea. This poem quotes words by the Chinese monk Shih T'ou (700–790).

HAN SHAN AND SHIH TE (PAGE 30)
These two are commonly depicted in a popular Chinese porcelain sculpture as two fat men rolling with laughter.

There are several legends about their encounter on the Chinese mountain where Han Shan was a Ch'an hermit.

ONE LITTLE KID (PAGE 34)
The Three Jewels *(Triratna)* of Buddhism are the Buddha, the Dharma (teaching), and the Sangha (community).

FRIENDS (PAGE 35)
Cape Kuryong is on, and Ullong Island some miles off, the east coast of Korea.

WHY KILL? (PAGE 36)
In the disciplines of Buddhism the call to break all ties with the world of phenomena is sometimes dramatized in such expressions as "kill Buddha if you meet him" or "kill your parents if you meet them."

BIRTHPLACE (PAGE 36)
Han Yong-Un (1879–1944) was a noted Buddhist monk, a poet, and novelist. He was one of the original signatories of the Declaration of Korean Independence of March 1, 1919.

TRIPITAKA KOREANA (PAGE 39)
This is the name given to the huge collection of Buddhist scriptures carved on over eighty thousand wooden blocks in the thirteenth century and now preserved at Haein Temple in central South Korea.

ANANDA (PAGE 39)
Ananda and Kashyapa are both mentioned in the oldest stories about the life of the historical Buddha, Shakyamuni, as being particularly close to the Master.

RECORDS OF THE TRANSMISSION OF THE LAMP (PAGE 40)
This is the title of a Chinese Ch'an treatise, the *Ching te Ch'uan teng lu,* written by Tao Yuan in the Sung Dynasty.

YEH FU (PAGE 40)
The *Diamond Sutra* is one of the major Mahayana Sutras. Its full name is *The Diamond-Cutter Perfection of Wisdom Sutra* or the *Vajracchedika* and it is a short version, made in the fourth century, of earlier *Prajñaparamita (Perfection of Wisdom) Sutras,* central to the Madhyamaka (Middle Way) School of philosophical Buddhism.

One part of the *Diamond Sutra* is entitled "Yeh Fu's Song," and the poem plays on the fact that there was a Chinese monk of that name, whose life history the poem evokes, in the eleventh century (1063 C.E.).

Parallax Press publishes books and tapes on mindful awareness and social responsibility, "making peace right in the moment we are alive."

For a copy of our free catalog, please write to:

Parallax Press
P.O. Box 7355
Berkeley, California 94707
www.parallax.org